MOBY 18

Piano Vocal Guitar

Published 2002
© International Music Publications Limited
Griffin house, 161 Hammersmith Road, London, W6 8BS, England

Edited by Chris Harvey
Music arranged by Artemis Music Ltd
Photography by Danny Clinch
Design by David Calderly
Folio design by Dominic Brookman

WE ARE ALL MADE OF STARS

Words and Music by Moby

1. Grow-ing in num-bers,   grow-ing in speed.—
2. Ef - forts of lov - ers   left in my mind.—
   (Verse 3 see block lyric)   I

Can't fight the fu - ture,   can't fight what I   see.—
sing in the reach-es   we'll see what we   find.—

Peo-ple they come to-ge-ther,_ and peo-ple they fall a - part._

No-one can stop us now_ 'cause we are all made of stars._

Peo-ple they come to-ge-ther,_ and peo-ple they fall a - part._

No-one can stop us now_ 'cause we are all made of stars._

To Coda ⊕

Vocal ad lib.

D.%. al Coda (no repeat)

Ev-en love is a go-ing round. You can't ig-nore what's go-ing round.

Coda

Peo-ple they come to-ge-ther, and peo-ple they fall a-part.

No-one can stop us now 'cause we are all made of stars.

Verse 3:
Slowly rebuilding,
I feel it in me.
Growing in numbers,
And growing in peace.

People, they come together *etc.*

IN THIS WORLD

Words and Music by Moby

IN MY HEART

Words and Music by Moby

GREAT ESCAPE

Words and Music by Moby, Orenda Fink and Maria Taylor

ONE OF THESE MORNINGS

Words and Music by Moby

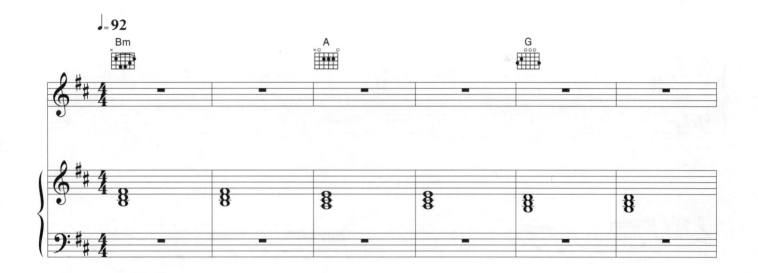

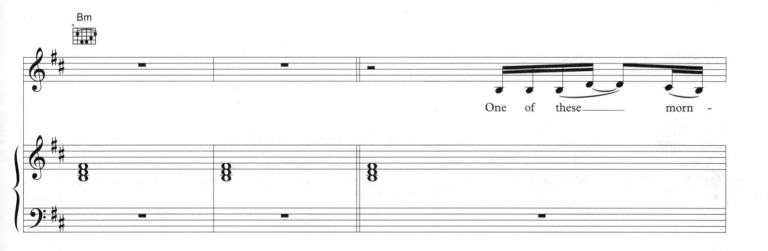

One of these_____ morn-

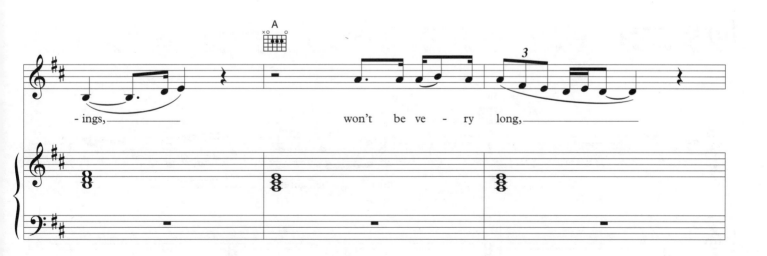

-ings,_____ won't be ve - ry long,_____

SIGNS OF LOVE

Words and Music by Moby

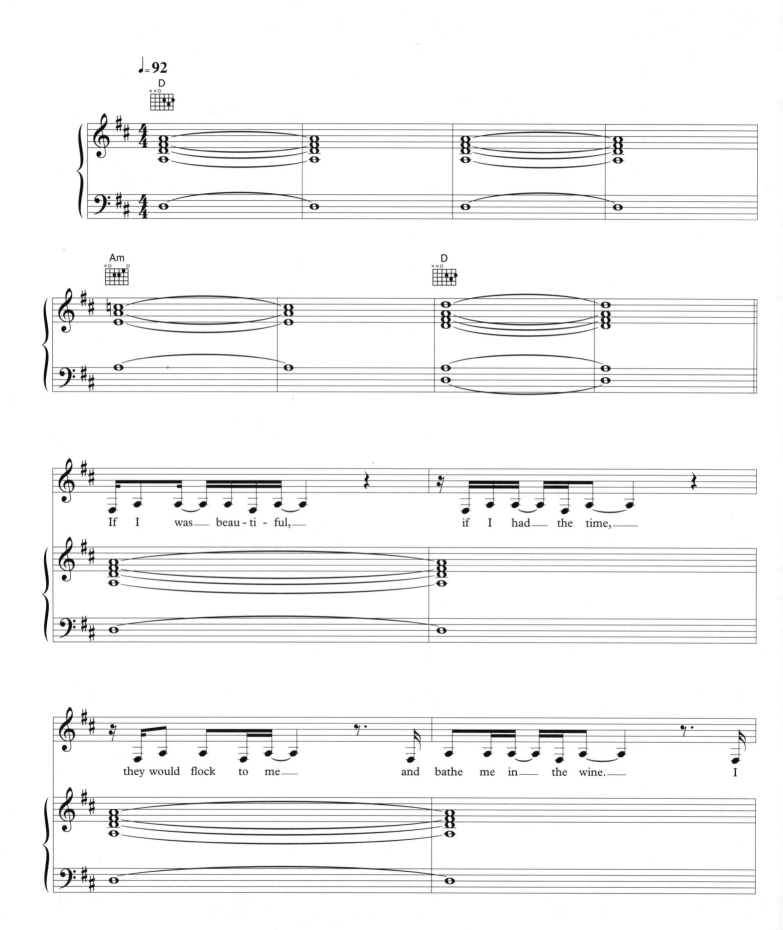

I can see__ the light__ come peer - ing through the sky__ in my__ mind.

Cra - zy peo - ple call__ me i - di - ot, al - so ly - ing on__ the floor.__

Am

I would hold__ you in__ my arms__ un - til we both are old.__

D

I would hold__ you in__ my arms__ un - til we both are all a - lone.__

ANOTHER WOMAN

Words and Music by Moby and Barbera Ozen

You got an-oth-er wo-man some - where a - round.

You leave your home for days and days. You leave your home for days

and days. You leave your home for days and days.

32

FIREWORKS

Words and Music by Moby

SUNDAY (THE DAY BEFORE MY BIRTHDAY)

Words and Music by Moby and Sylvia Robinson

Sun-day was a bright day yes-ter-day.

Dark cloud has come in-to the way.

Sun-day was a bright day yes-ter-day.

EXTREME WAYS

Words and Music by Moby

Verse 3:
Extreme sounds that told me
They helped me down every night
I didn't have much to say
I didn't give up the life
I closed my eyes and closed myself
And closed my world and never opened up to anything
It couldn't get me at all.

Verse 4:
I had to close down everything
I had to close down my mind
Too many things should cover me
Too much could make me blind
I've seen so much in so many places
So many heartaches, so many faces
So many dirty things
You couldn't even believe.

I would stand in line for this
It's always good in life for this.

Oh baby, *etc.*

JAM FOR THE LADIES

Words and Music by Moby, Michael McDermon, Angie Stone,
Lana Morrer, Robert James and Mark Sparks

Fly from the top to the bottom; it's gonna be "cut 'em, gut 'em, we got 'em!" It's like the old leagues. It's a

jam for the lad-ies and a su - per-star;— I could lead the whole set but nev-er go too far.— It's a

jam for the lad-ies and a su - per-star;— I could lead the whole set but nev-er go too far.— It's a

jam for the lad-ies and a su - per-star;— I could lead the whole set but nev-er go too far.—

Take you from where-ev-er to where-ev- er you are.....

Take you from where-ev-er to where-ev- er you are.....

Take you from where-ev-er to where-ev- er you are.....

Take you from where-ev-er to where-ev- er you are.....

(Spoken) You know I can't stand to be held back.   And all the ladies, y'all get off my back, yeah.   Even when we're solo in action,

we come together like six set o' Jacksons.   Jam for the ladies and a superstar.   Lyte lead the set but never go too far.

I toured the world, but I'm rolling it now. Don't want my girl to brag, but Eve was holding it down, now.

Jam for the ladies, and we putting you down; 'cause we're snatching the crown, 'cause we fend for high ground. It's a

jam for the lad-ies and a su - per-star;— I could lead the whole set but nev-er go too far.— It's a

Play 6 times

jam for the ladies and a su-per-star; I could lead the whole set but never go too far. It's a jam for the ladies and a superstar.—

18

Words and Music by Moby

SLEEP ALONE

Words and Music by Moby

AT LEAST WE TRIED

Words and Music by Moby

HARBOUR

Words and Music by Moby

street bears no re-lief _____ when
(2.) run the stairs a-way _____ and
(Verses 3 & 4 see block lyrics)

1. The

Verse 3:
The heat is on its own
The roof seems so inviting
A vantage point is gained
To watch the children fighting.

Verse 4:
So lead me to the harbour
And float me on the waves
Sink me in the ocean
To sleep in a sailor's grave
To sleep in a sailor's grave.

My heart is full *etc.*

THE RAFTERS

Words and Music by Moby

LOOK BACK IN

Words and Music by Moby

I'M NOT WORRIED AT ALL

Words and Music by Moby